ideals®
MOTHER'S DAY

MARCH 2003

Dedicated to a celebration—through poetry and prose—of the American ideals of faith in God, loyalty to country, and love of family.

God shows that He is everywhere by the triumph and power of a mother's love.
—Author Unknown

IDEALS—Vol. 60, No. 2 March 2003 IDEALS (ISSN 0019-137X, USPS 256-240) is published six times a year: January, March, May, July, September, and November by IDEALS PUBLICATIONS, a division of Guideposts, 39 Seminary Hill Road, Carmel, NY 10512. Copyright © 2003 by IDEALS PUBLICATIONS, a division of Guideposts. All rights reserved. The cover and entire contents of IDEALS are fully protected by copyright and must not be reproduced in any manner whatsoever. Title IDEALS registered U.S. Patent Office. Printed and bound in USA by Quebecor Printing. Printed on Weyerhaeuser Husky. The paper used in this publication meets the minimum requirements of American National Standard for Information Sciences—Permanence of Paper for Printed Library Materials, ANSI Z39.48-1984. Periodicals postage paid at Carmel, New York, and additional mailing offices. POSTMASTER: Send address changes to Ideals, 39 Seminary Hill Road, Carmel, NY 10512. For subscription or customer service questions, contact Ideals Publications, a division of Guideposts, 39 Seminary Hill Road, Carmel, NY 10512. Fax 845-228-2115. Reader Preference Service: We occasionally make our mailing lists available to other companies whose products or services might interest you. If you prefer not to be included, please write to Ideals Customer Service.

ISBN 0-8249-1206-3 GST 893989236

Visit the *Ideals* website at www.idealsbooks.com

Cover photo: Spring bouquet. Photo by Nancy Matthews/Robertstock.com.
Inside Front Cover: JUST BEGINNERS *by artist Shelly Reeves Smith. Image courtesy of Main Street Press, Ltd.*
Inside Back Cover: THE FIRST BORN *by artist Marie Aimee Lucas. Image from Christie's Images.*

In This Issue

Streets of May

Clara M. Morrison

Memory rode with me today,
Taking me over the streets of May,
Wafting a fragrance from bud and bloom,
Lilac and apple and peach perfume.
Watching the willows lean down and sway,
Memory listened with me today—
To the robin's sonata, the song sparrow's trill,
As we rounded the curve to the orchard hill.

Memory saw a small roan horse
Pulling a carriage over the course,
Pausing to drink near a wayside stream
Where a trough was built from a farmer's dream.

There bounteous blossoms festooned the trees,
And a nectar sweetness perfumed the breeze.
For always there lives in the months of spring
Fragrance and beauty to make the heart sing,
To store in the mind as a honeybee
Saves its sweets in a hollow tree.
So much my memory said today
As it rode with me over the streets of May.

*Crab-apple blossoms shelter the street
leading to a covered bridge near Parfreyville,
Wisconsin. Photo by Ken Dequaine.*

May Music

George N. Rees

I sing of glamorous magic of the glorious May
That greets glad morning on the misty peaks,
That glances boldly at the hastening noon,
And mingles splendor with the setting sun
When twilight's tender hush subdues the day
With muted symphonies of evening glow,
From which there drifts a thrush's lullaby
Deep in the happy heart of peaceful hills.

I sing of starry wonder of the friendly night,
Pleasantly cool, divinely beautiful.
Thence many a trail has led to happiness.
The rugged swain now hurries to his maid;
The family saunters toward the meeting house;
The fisher tensely feels the long, taut line;
The hunter hears the yapping of a fox—
Momentous joys in eternal hills.

I sing of mossy cliffs and valleys green
Where snowy flocks now gambol on the lea,
Where gentle cattle lick their glossy sides,
Where plots of clover buzz with busy bees,
Where field and forest stir with newborn life,
And where the murmuring streams
        of living, crystal waters
Send softest echoes in my dreams forever,
Their notes resounding through enchanted hills.

I sing of maples decked with silver leaves,
Of cedars giving incense of delight,
Of sturdy oaks that shelter and protect,
Of spreading elms where twitter fledgling birds.
And these, the trees, cry out in holy praise;
The fragrant meadows hum with sweet applause.
The little people of the forest dance
To May's gay music in the singing hills.

*Left: Wildflowers adorn a hillside in Washington's
Olympic National Park. Photo by Dianne Dietrich Leis.
Overleaf: Tulips line a gentle stream in Louisiana's
Hodges Garden. Photo by Dick Dietrich.*

Spring

Esther Kem Thomas

When God created earth and sky
And all things in between
And tried out each new element,
I know He must have seen
That after winter's sealed-up length
The earth should wake and sing.
Yes, with His understanding eyes
He saw and gave us spring.

Far-seeing, too, He knew in spring
How boys need trees to climb
And girls need skates, how fingers
Harden up at marble time,
How neighbor-talk gets friendly like.
He saw to everything!
As though He couldn't prove enough
His love, He gave us spring.

With gentle hands, the daffodils
He wooed and touched to green
The yonder hills and smiled upon
The skies, new-washed and clean.
And to the birds He whispered, "Come,
Lift up your hearts and sing!"
And hope and faith surge up anew
Because God gave us spring.

Spring

Vera B. Hammann

Afar the trees on yonder slope
Are touched with pink and white,
While dashes of pale lavender
Of lilacs burst in sight.
As if upon the highest peak
Where Nature holds her sway,
She tossed across the grassy hills
A many-flowered bouquet;
And, caught up in the gentle wind,
She scattered here and there
The lovely blooms of springtime
To make the earth more fair.
Close-grown beside the garden walks,
Gay tulips catch the breeze,
While robins spill their joyousness
In fresh, green-budding trees.
'Tis May again, and young and old
Greet the awakening;
For deep within their hearts they share
The glory of the spring.

A branch from an apple tree droops across a picket fence in Alpine, Oregon. Photo by Dennis Frates.

From My Garden Journal

GRAPE HYACINTH

Laurie Hunter

When I moved to a new house a few months ago, I was eager to get started on a flower garden. The dismal yard was devoid of color—more than an acre with merely one tree and a vast expanse of grass. As a watercolorist, a garden is a necessity, just as important as a kitchen; it is inspiring to be surrounded by beauty, and flowers always seem eager to pose for a painting. So I began by planting something easy: a cheerful, spring-flowering herb, the grape hyacinth. I planted the bulbs under our solitary tree, where they will be the foundation underneath future plants that will require more direct sunlight.

How spectacular this corner of my yard looks now that spring has arrived! A solid blanket of blue grape hyacinths stretches beneath the formerly meager tree, and these generous beauties will give me brilliant blue blooms for weeks.

Grape hyacinths are some of the easiest bulbs to grow because they are so hardy. A plant of the genus *Muscari armeniacum*, the grape hyacinth is not a true hyacinth. Instead, it is a perennial bulb belonging to the lily family. Look closely at its flowers, though, and you will see similarities to hyacinths: clustered tiny flowers and grasslike

> *With showy blue, grapelike flowers, this plant is perfect for adding a natural feeling to impromptu garden paths created by the scurrying of little toddler feet.*

foliage. With a graceful, leafless stem and showy blue, grapelike flowers, this plant is perfect for edging borders and adding a natural feeling to impromptu garden paths created by the scurrying of little toddler feet that frequently accompany me in my garden.

The grape hyacinth's name can be traced back to the Greek mythological story of a boy named Hyacinth who was killed when a discus hit his head. While lying in the arms of the grieving god Apollo, the flower sprang from the cut on Hyacinth's head. The plants were first found growing in 1573 in Turkey, when a visiting German doctor collected samples of the blooms to take back to Europe. By the early 1700s, they were very popular.

GRAPE HYACINTH

Some gardeners actually consider grape hyacinths to be weeds. Such a notion is completely abandoned when the gardener is also an artist. True, their stems are unabashedly grasslike. These stems, however, only add to the easygoing charm of the swaying clusters of tiny purple bells.

There are approximately fifty species of grape hyacinth. The colors of their petals range from blue to purple, which explains the "grape" part of their name. I believe their sweet scent even smells a bit grapey. The grape hyacinth is sometimes called the starch hyacinth because some say the flowers smell like wet starch. In fact, the name of the genus, *Muscari*, comes from the Greek word for musk, an aroma emitted by some species.

An excellent New Year's Day tradition is to plant the bulbs in the ground in the middle of winter. It's a bleak time of year to be outside, no doubt. Your reward for freezing your fingers to the bone will come to you around mid-February or March. Don't panic if a late snowfall surprises your grape hyacinth plantings in April. They can withstand the chill and will reassure you by shining brightly against any unforeseen wintry precipitation.

Grape hyacinth bulbs can be forced indoors in temperatures of around 60° F in a bright room. If they droop, the plants may be too warm or are not getting enough indirect light.

Be warned that rodents like to dig up and eat newly planted grape hyacinth bulbs. Therefore, I usually plant mine with daffodils or scilla bulbs, both of which are disliked by rodents. The resulting composite of cheery blooms secretes a good deal of nectar, making them appealing to bees in the spring. Other flowers that bloom well with grape hyacinths include sweet William, foxglove, baby's breath, coralberry, and (surprise!) dandelions. Also often considered a weed, dandelions bloom simultaneously with grape hyacinth blooms. If you plant grape hyacinth bulbs throughout your lawn in winter, you'll soon create a dazzling dandelion yellow and hyacinth purple show of complementary colors—an artist's delight!

Because grape hyacinths are relatively small, they make the greatest impact when planted in large groupings. Simply slice the soil with a trowel about five or six inches deep, drop in the bulbs three to four inches apart, and replace the scattered soil to cover the bulbs. If the idea of planting hundreds of bulbs in the dead of winter sounds daunting, consider this: each takes only seconds to plant if your soil is loose. Within a couple of hours, the job will be done, and you'll be intensely satisfied with the anticipation of spring.

Grape hyacinths need partial to full sun and will bloom from five to ten inches tall, depending on the variety, from March through May. Keep in mind that grape hyacinths eagerly multiply when you aren't looking. So plant them where they can feel free to roam with abandon. A meadow is ideal, or under groupings of shrubbery. Resist any urge to confine grape hyacinths to formal flower beds. They will only disappoint with their unruly spirit and sprawl. To prevent the bulbs from protruding from the ground after several years of being planted, mulch the planting with two to four inches of bark.

Just as the first early-blooming bulbs signal the beginning of spring, a garden freshly planted at a new home ushers in a new chapter of life. All the boxes that were once towering in my family's new house have been unpacked and our belongings put in order. As I look outside my window to the blooming grape hyacinths, I am inspired to begin a new watercolor; and I realize that our new place is beginning to feel like home.

Laurie Hunter lives with her family in Leiper's Fork, Tennessee, where young Alexis and Oliver love to follow her through the garden.

EARLY SPRING
Susan Allen Toth

*E*arly spring was probably the most exciting time in the North Woods, for then Mother took us to hunt for May-basket flowers. On a chilly Saturday morning when the sun finally broke from gray skies into the thin, clear sunshine of early spring, Mother hung an old willow basket over her arm and led my sister and me to a hidden entrance into the woods a half mile away from our house. Down a winding path, barely visible under the last patches of melting snow and moldy leaves, we followed Mother's sure steps, looking carefully as we walked for nearby flowers. Mother taught us how to find the delicate white Dutchman's breeches and snowdrops, and we gathered them into small bouquets with wild purple violets. We soon turned to scamper home, running ahead of her now, yelling and racing while she followed slowly with the picnic basket full of flowers. When we got home, we had hot rolls and cocoa while we constructed little baskets out of colored paper to fill with flowers and lace at our neighbors' doors.

A woodland walk yields a basket of blooms in Anthonore Christensen's painting ANEMONES AND PRIMROSES IN A BASKET. *Image from Eaton Gallery, Princes Arcade/Fine Art Photographic Library, London/Art Resource, New York.*

Bits and Pieces

*T*o a certain extent we raise a garden as we might a child, putting in the seed, nourishing it and gathering nourishment from it, pruning and weeding its growth, protecting it, loving it, worrying over it.

—Robert Finch

*W*hat is a weed? A plant whose virtues have not yet been discovered.

—Ralph Waldo Emerson

*D*ear common flower, that grow'st beside the way,
Fringing the dusty road with harmless gold; . . .
Though art more dear to me
Than all the prouder summer blooms may be.

—James Russell Lowell

*N*othing like weeding to unknot the mind.

—May Sarton

*B*ut make no mistake, the weeds will win: nature bats last.

—Robert Michael Pyle

She loved everything that grew in God's earth, even the weeds. With one exception. If she found a blade of nut grass in her yard, it was like the Second Battle of the Marne.

—Harper Lee

To move down a line of flowers, inch by inch, pulling weeds, and to be able an hour or two later—who could tell how much time had passed?—to look back and see the flowers standing by themselves against the brown soil, gave me a feeling of joy different from any I had known.

—Jay Neugeboren

It takes me longer to weed than most people, because I will do it so thoroughly. It is such a pleasure and satisfaction to clear the beautiful brown earth, smooth and soft.

—Celia Thaxter

No garden is without its weeds.

—Thomas Fuller

I guess a good gardener always starts as a good weeder.

—Amos Pettingill

The great wonder, in gardening, is that so many plants live.

—Christopher Lloyd

15

Boy Flying Kite
Annette Victorin

He holds a ball of gold-spun string tied to
A star he borrowed from a shining night.
It patterns in the sky, as dreams glow through
Bright castles clinging to his rugged kite.
This is his world, this prairie choked with weeds.
The wind-broomed sky, so clean, smiles down at him.
These are the moments that, like vital seeds,
Will sprout slim rainbows when the years grow dim.
Nothing on earth can match his joyous mood.
His ships are white; his men walk firm and straight.
This dew-drenched dawn is but an interlude
That helps unwind his golden thread and fate.
Oh, may he always keep this blue-eyed day
To lean upon when thunder comes his way.

Early Lesson
Anna Holm Pogue

With long degree of patience in the doing,
We children of the valley made a kite.
And gusty springtime came and lifted it
Above the orchard trees, above the vane
On the highest peak of the barn. A captive gull,
It pulled against the slender cord until
Our upflung arms could meet the strain no more.
Despairingly we watched it sail away
Beyond the budding trees, beyond the hills,
Dim to the sight and gone, with no return.
On reaching home with hardly stifled sobs,
"Alas our precious kite is gone. Is gone!"
"You must not grieve, you should be very proud;
For kites are made to fly. Yours did not fail!
Not many have the skill to build a kite
Which comes to life and trails the string away."

A kite-flyer enjoys the spring winds in Portland, Oregon. Photo by Steve Terrill.

Glorified Bouquet

Gail Elder James

They came, three little boys from down the street,
And rapped upon my door.
Three tiny lads, half shy, and I'm not sure
I'd seen the three before.

But there they stood, and in each little hand
A bunch of dandelions.
"These are for you," they said, and time gave back
Three little boys of mine.

They brought me dandelions in early spring,
Their gift on Mother's Day.
How strange yet sweet, this humble flower
Became a glorified bouquet.

Love Affair

Madeleine Laeufer

The loveliest flowers along my way,
From prom corsage to bride's bouquet,
Have been eclipsed by a dusty nosegay—

Clover blossoms and Queen Anne's lace,
Given to me with a warm embrace
And a proud, happy smile on a small, dirty face.

My eyes spill the joy which my heart can't hold.
More precious to me than orchids of gold,
These backyard blooms from my three-year-old.

Florist

Esther Kem Thomas

It was a beautiful corsage!
She made it, squatting on one knee,
Intently counting, "One, two, fee."
She was so careful to arrange
Each flower in her hand. How strange
That three stemless violets

Resembling drooping, shy vignettes;
Two dandelions; a strand of grass
Could, by their giving, so surpass
An orchid! There by the garage
She knelt to fashion my corsage.

A mother receives a gift from the heart on the shore of Boston's Charles River. Photo by Dianne Dietrich Leis.

Mother

Emma Ruth Yoder
Meyersville, Pennsylvania

There is no other one on earth
Who'd fill my mother's place;
She's always gentle, kind, and true
And wears a smiling face.

She dried my tears when I was small
And bandaged many hurts;
She tenderly would clean me up
When I fell in the dirt.

So lovingly she cared for me
And often gave a kiss
When childish troubles loomed up high
And too when I was sick.

At night she got up many times
To feed and care for me;
And even though she too was tired,
She'd first look out for me.

She'd lovingly caress me when
I thought that no one cared.
She hugged me tight and soothingly
Would often send up prayers.

So through it all the bonds did grow
Between my mom and me,
And so I say she is the best
And dearest still to me.

Readers' Reflections

Readers are invited to submit original poetry for possible publication in future issues of Ideals. *Please send typed copies only; manuscripts will not be returned. Writers receive $10 for each published submission. Send material to Readers' Reflections, Ideals Publications, 535 Metroplex Drive, Suite 250, Nashville, Tennessee 37211.*

Little Eyes

C. David Hay
Rosedale, Indiana

Oh, to see the world again
Through the eyes of a tiny child,
To marvel at the mysteries
Of all things tamed and wild:

The blossom of a flower,
Bright diamonds in the snow,
To watch the flight of birds
And dream of where they go;

The dance of dainty butterflies,
Trees that touch the sky,
Enchantment of all creatures
That run or swim or fly.

Countless thrills are awaiting
The touch of a tiny hand;
Adventure's just a step away
In the place called wonderland.

Every road is one not taken;
Each day brings a new surprise.
God must have made this all
Just for little eyes.

Where Will Your Footsteps Run?

Jenna Mosley
Duncan, Arizona

Dear little babe, our darling son,
Asleep in your cradle, life just begun.
Tiny, sweet feet under the sheet.
Where will your footsteps run?

Dearest toddler, two or three,
Your heart is happy, full of glee.
Feet are growing; eyes are glowing.
Where will your footsteps run?

Dear first grader, much taller now,
Ready for all the world will allow.
Feet are secure; they will endure.
Where will your footsteps run?

High school grad, handsome and tall:
"Here I come, world; I hear your call."
May you find joy, our precious boy,
Wherever your footsteps run.

Happy Mother's Day

Martha Nighswander
Barwick, Ontario

Mother dear, this is your special day.
And I, your little girl, am far away.
But in my dreams and in my heart and mind,
I still can feel your loving arms so kind
Around me, and it gives me comfort too
To know your prayers are constant and so true.
On Mother's Day I'll long to see your face,
But surely God will give sufficient grace.
His love so great surrounds both you and me
And keeps us close, though miles between us be.
His spirit in us keeps our courage high.
As you serve there and I serve here, He's nigh.
I thank Him for your life, faithful and true,
That makes me want to serve our Jesus too.
May God to you this day assurance give
That life is yet worthwhile for you to live.
May He to your dear mother-heart give peace
And joy and blessings that will never cease.

Kindred Souls

Linda Ward
Eureka, California

Two such kindred souls as we
Mother and daughter had to be.
We both love to hear the rain
Pelt against the windowpane.

When setting sun paints the sky,
We watch in wonder, you and I.
Whene'er we read poetry,
We feel the same intensity.

Our joy comes from the everyday—
The sparrow's song, a child at play.
The good Lord knew two souls as we
Mother and daughter had to be.

Mothers
Margaret Rorke

Dear God, please bless the mom today
Who holds upon her knee
The child who'll lead all folks to pray—
The minister-to-be.

Bless her who's bandaging the thumb
Of him whose tears are thick,
Of him who in the days to come
Will heal his fellow sick.

Bless her who carries him about
While shopping shelf by shelf.
Someday the squirming little sprout
Will own a store himself.

Bless her who hears her own recite
His homework or his speech,
Who knows that he must get it right
Because someday he'll teach.

Bless her whose interest proves for him
The catalyst he needs
To follow forth with all his vim
Great scientific leads.

Bless her who cheers when he's at bat—
The sandlot's pride and joy—
'Cause time will make him more than that;
He'll be a big-league boy.

God, bless their efforts day by day.
Assist in all they do,
For this old world in every way
Depends on them and You.

Blocks build an afternoon of fun in CHILD PLAYING
*by artist Frances Foy. Image from National
Museum of American Art, Smithsonian Institution,
Washington, D.C./Art Resource, New York.*

Ideals' Family Recipes

Many moms have been awakened on Mother's Day morning by a grinning little one holding a paper plate full of overdone toast. Although the grin makes up for the lack of culinary expertise, Mom is sure to enjoy one of the great breakfast treats below, as long as they are still served with a smile. We would love to try your favorite recipe too. Send a typed copy to Ideals Publications, 535 Metroplex Drive, Suite 250, Nashville, TN 37211. We pay $10 for each recipe published.

Apple Breakfast Cake

Barb Marshall of Pickerington, Ohio

3½ cups all-purpose flour	2 eggs, slightly beaten
1 cup plus 3 tablespoons granulated sugar, divided	1 cup plus 2 tablespoons water
2 teaspoons baking powder	2 cups finely chopped apple
¾ teaspoon salt	2¼ teaspoons cinnamon
½ cup shortening	1½ tablespoons melted butter

Preheat oven to 400° F. In a large bowl, sift together flour, 3 tablespoons of the sugar, baking powder, and salt. Cut in shortening and mix well. Add eggs and water. Mix to make a soft dough. Spread dough evenly into a greased, 9-by-13-by-2-inch baking dish. In a medium bowl, combine remaining 1 cup sugar, apple, cinnamon, and butter; spread evenly over top of dough. Bake 25 to 30 minutes. Makes 12 servings.

Breakfast Casserole

Marguerite Lebert of Ontario, Canada

2 cups frozen hash browns	8 eggs
½ cup green pepper, chopped	½ cup milk
¼ cup green onion, chopped	¼ teaspoon dry mustard
1 tablespoon dried parsley	1 cup cooked, diced ham
2 tablespoons butter	1 cup shredded Cheddar cheese

Preheat oven to 400° F. In a large skillet over medium heat, combine first 5 ingredients and sauté until hash browns are slightly golden. Remove from heat and set aside. In a large mixing bowl, beat together eggs, milk, and dry mustard. Add ham and cheese; mix well. Stir in hash brown mixture. Pour into a lightly greased, 9-by-13-by-2-inch baking dish. Bake 17 to 22 minutes or until eggs are set. Makes 8 servings.

The Closest Cookie

Margaret Rorke

I began to talk of manners,
And the one I'd advocate
With particular attention
To a certain cookie plate
That I just had finished passing.
What was once a stately stack
With dispatch became the vestige
Of a juvenile attack.

"It's polite to take the closest
As the cookies come around,
With no eye to size or raisins"
Was my lesson most profound

For the little group of munchers;
And I feared it made no hit
Till one asked, "Is it politeness
If we turn the plate a bit?"

Now, an etiquette compiler
Would deny the course he sought,
But beyond the flush of humor
Lies a philosophic thought:
Few of us accept the meager
As we take the dish of fate.
If the better lies beyond us,
We attempt to turn the plate.

*Story time is always more fun with something
to nibble. Photo by Jessie Walker.*

Baked Pancake

E. Meigs of East Aurora, New York

⅓ cup all-purpose flour

⅛ teaspoon cinnamon

⅛ teaspoon nutmeg

1 egg

2 teaspoons granulated sugar

2 drops vanilla extract

½ cup milk

2 tablespoons butter

Preheat oven to 375° F. In a medium mixing bowl, sift together flour, cinnamon, and nutmeg. Set aside. In a large mixing bowl, combine egg, sugar, vanilla extract, and milk. Slowly stir in dry ingredients and mix well. Set aside. In an 8-inch, ovenproof skillet, melt butter over medium heat until bubbly. Quickly pour all batter into the pan and place in oven. Bake 8 to 10 minutes or until pancake is golden brown and firm. Before serving, top center of pancake with powdered sugar, fruit, or jam. Serve immediately. Makes 1 serving.

Breakfast Fruit Drink

Karene Kerman of Grand Rapids, Michigan

2 bananas, sliced

2 cups orange juice

2 cups pineapple juice

In a blender, combine all ingredients until smooth. Makes 4 servings.

Savory Biscuits

Linda Giles of Boothbay, Maine

3 cups all-purpose flour

⅛ cup baking powder

1 tablespoon dried parsley

1 teaspoon garlic powder

¾ teaspoon salt

1 stick butter, softened

1¼ cups buttermilk

Preheat oven to 425° F. In a medium mixing bowl, sift together flour, baking powder, parsley, garlic powder, and salt. Cut in butter until mixture resembles coarse crumbs. Stir in buttermilk and mix until soft dough forms. Roll dough out approximately ¼ inch thick on a floured surface. Using a biscuit cutter, cut out biscuits and place on a greased cookie sheet. Bake 15 minutes. Makes approximately 16 biscuits.

Mothers

Author Unknown

I think God took the fragrance of a flower,
A pure white flower which blooms not for world praise
But which makes sweet and beautiful some bower;
The compassion of the dew, which gently lays
Reviving freshness on the fainting earth
And gives to all the tired things new birth;
The steadfastness and radiance of stars
Which lift the soul above the confining bar;
The gladness of fair dawns; the sunset's peace;
Contentment which from "trivial rounds" asks no release;
The life which finds its greatest joy in deeds of love for others—
I think God took these precious things and made of them the mothers.

The angels, whispering to one another,
Can find, among their burning
terms of love,
None so devotional as that of "mother."

—EDGAR ALLAN POE

*Roses fill the air with fragrance in a garden in
Salem, Oregon. Photo by Dianne Dietrich Leis.*

Susan Meets Spring

Betty Stuart

I'm having lots of fun this spring
Acquainting Sue with everything.
This April is her first, you know;
She was not here a year ago.

"This is forsythia," I say
And let her sniff the golden spray.
"That lovely green is grass, small one,
That glory overhead is sun!

"The flash of scarlet is a bird;
He sang that lovely song you heard.
That gentle breeze that touched your cheek
Is April playing hide-and-seek.

"This is a leaf, and that's a tree
Where apple blossoms soon will be."
Sue looks intently and with pleasure
On all this newfound worldly treasure.

I've seen the springtime come and go
For forty years; but as I show
It to this baby's eyes of blue,
To her and me it's all brand new.

*A toddler enjoys her special reading rock in an
Illinois garden. Photo by Jessie Walker.*

THROUGH MY WINDOW

OH, BABY!

We visited a family restaurant in Seattle last summer, and I got the dubious honor of waiting in the drizzle while my husband retrieved the car from a few blocks away. By the time he returned, I had received an education in a subject I had no idea even existed—baby chic! Since that time I've been a keen observer of babies and young families, and I have determined this is not strictly a Pacific Northwestern phenomenon. It's everywhere. It could just be the new trend of the twenty-first century!

Remember, not too long ago, when having a baby meant picking up some diapers and a few kimonos, some booties, and maybe one of those cute little baby towels with the hood thing in the corner? And then if we needed a stroller or a car seat, we scrounged around to see who had a secondhand one we could use. Hand-me-down clothes worked really well, too, because what baby ever wore out little smocked dresses or appliquéd rompers? If that's how you recall baby accessories, you're as out of it as I was. It's a whole new world out there now.

In the ten minutes I spent waiting outside the spaghetti restaurant, I counted at least six different stroller models. Some of them had so many handles, levers, pads, and straps you could hardly see the baby. I watched one intelligent-looking young man for about five minutes as he tried to figure out how to transform his baby car seat into a stroller. There appeared to be several transitional stages to this particular item. As near as I could tell, you could use it for a carrier, car seat, bed, stroller, highchair—maybe even a space capsule! It was all chrome with rolled and pleated upholstery and looked like it cost more than our first car.

And let me tell you, these babies weren't dressed in any hand-me-downs either. They had color-coordinated denim outfits embroidered with famous logos. Little tykes who couldn't even walk were decked out in trendy miniature athletic shoes.

And if they got fussy while waiting for their dinner reservation, these tots sure weren't bored. Modern mommies and daddies don't use rattles or car keys to entertain their children. Oh my, no. They have entire educational play sets tucked away in designer diaper bags. One woman set up what I can only describe as a baby entertainment center right there in front the restaurant. She clipped some dangly plastic shapes on one side of the stroller so they extended over the baby's face, yanked on a string that started music, and then propped up a fold-out book of black-and-white portraits for her infant to study. Another mother spent her downtime rehearsing a series of sign language gestures with her tiny offspring. At first I thought maybe the child was hearing-impaired, but then I overheard the mother say that learning sign language "improves the

> *Modern mommies and daddies have entire educational play sets tucked away in designer diaper bags.*

baby's cognitive development by enhancing his communicative skills, thus alleviating his preverbal frustration." Huh? Whatever happened to pat-a-cake and peekaboo?

Once I got home I decided to do a bit of research on this subject and I found out some other amazing things about baby accouterments in the new millennium. Do you know that you can order a real British pram? Not just any pram, but the genuine Silver Stream Pram by Silver Cross, which has "a coach body finished with fine lining, an English leather suspension, and painted steel chassis." Better hurry though. The free shipping offer only lasts for a limited time—and you'll need it, because the price tag is twenty-one hundred dollars.

But what if you don't want to go perambulating around the neighborhood? What if you just want to stay at home with the new little family addition? Well, I sure hope you have a decorating plan. No more plunking a crib in the corner of the bedroom. Today there are baby decorators out there just itching to turn your nursery into a work of art. Because, as you probably already know, "the days of the single hanging mobile are gone— today's parents entertain through design." Before

you call up the decorator, however, you may want to decide what style your baby will find most nurturing. Some options are: contemporary, traditional, Italian influence, Victorian mix, or shabby chic. I particularly liked the definition offered under Italian: "Newborns are swept away in rich colors and grand décor, silk accents and opulent charm." I, on the other hand, was swept away by memories of my second newborn who frequently dampened or spit up on any décor within a two-foot radius, opulent or not.

Yes, it's a brand new world out there for contemporary mommies, and they'll want to document every moment of their baby's life. But guess what? They don't even have to wait until their precious little bundle arrives. Anticipating consumers while they're still in the womb, several enterprising companies have set up studios where expectant mothers can get framed, 3-D photos of their unborn babies! Using ultrasound technology, the prints are produced in about thirty minutes—or if you're willing to wait for a week or so, you can get an in-utero video complete with background music. Think about how much fun you'd have with that when the first boyfriend comes to call!

I have no idea where all this will lead, but I'm tempted to see if the baby decorator does living rooms. And although I have some serious doubts about the designer baby trend, I do have faith that the babies aren't as impressed by it as their parents. As I stood in the drizzle watching that frustrated father wrestle with his super-high-tech stroller, I noticed that his infant son had dozed off peacefully in the oldest and simplest child carrier of all, his mother's arms.

Pamela Kennedy is a freelance writer of short stories, articles, essays, and children's books. Wife of a retired naval officer and mother of three children, she has made her home on both U.S. coasts and currently resides in Honolulu, Hawaii.

A SLICE OF LIFE

MOTHER'S SMILE

Edna Jaques

Mothers smile at each other here,
Over a baby's sleepy head,
A look as old as the life of man.
No matter what needless words are said,
A flash as deep as the human race
Has passed like a light from face to face.

For mothers know how a baby feels
Tucked in close to a tender cheek.
It's a language as old as the human race
That only the mothers of children speak,
The satin softness of hands and feet,
The rosy curve of its little seat.

Mothers know how your heart can freeze
At the thought of danger for little ones,
How precious a tiny girl can be,
The pride of a woman in bearing sons,
How empty a life can be, and cold,
Without a child of your own to hold.

Mothers smile at each other still.
Smiles that cover so much, so much
Love and faith and a little house,
Fingers of fear that sometimes clutch
At your heart's deep core where your feelings lie
Too deep for the eyes of a passerby.

Yet mothers smile o'er a baby's head
And understand though no words are said.

Robert Duncan began painting at age eleven, when his grandmother gave him his first set of oil paints. Today, Robert, his wife, his six children, and a lively assortment of farm animals live in the little town of Midway, Utah.

A mother and child share a garden walk in SPRING *by artist Robert Duncan. Image provided by Robert Duncan Studios.*

A Mother's Prayer

Betty W. Stoffel

Since Thou hast dared to trust me with
This life's supremest good,
Let me be found trustworthy in
The guard of motherhood.

Keep me in touch with Thy great love,
Patient, sure, and wise,
That I, in seeing earthly deeds,
May look with heaven's eyes.

Redeem the faults of thought and deed,
Each poor example set.
Uphold me for the sake of little
Minds that don't forget.

Teach me to balance love between
Too little and too much,
Yet to maintain in all of life
The outward-going touch.

Be Thou my courage, strength of heart,
My soul's up-reaching way
That little feet which follow mine
May not be led astray.

*A mother and daughter make a memory among the flow-
ers in* PLEASANT HOURS *by artist Edward Killingworth
Johnson. Image from Christie's Images.*

The Creation of Mothers

Henry Ward Beecher

When God thought of mother,
He must have laughed with satisfaction
and framed it quickly—
so rich, so deep, so divine,
so full of soul, power, and beauty
was the conception.

What Is a Mother?

G. Newell Lovejoy

God thought to give the sweetest thing
In His almighty power
To earth; and deeply pondering
What it should be—one hour
In fondest joy and love of heart
Outweighing every other—
He moved the gates of heaven apart
And gave to earth a mother!

Border: Pink azaleas brighten the landscape at Audubon Park in Louisville, Kentucky. Photo by Daniel Dempster. Inset right: A mother horse nuzzles her foal. Photo by M. Barrett/H. Armstrong Roberts.

Mother's Sunbonnet
C. C. Cuzzort

I recall the blue sunbonnet
That my mother always wore
When in the heat of summer's sun
She walked to a country store.

There was a pert, starched visor,
Her eyes and face to shade,
With tie-on ribbons at each side
That toil-worn hands had made.

When at last her steps turned westward
And all market trips were done,
That blue bonnet seemed to vanish
In a glorious setting sun.

Mother's Sunbonnets
Mary Joan Boyer

They were made of gingham or calico,
Ruffled and washed and ironed just so,
With a bow in back like a butterfly
And nice wide strings in front to tie.
Each one, as neat as the one before,
Hung in its place by the kitchen door,
Waiting for Mother to wear on her head
Whenever chickens had to be fed
Or there was some wash to hang on the line
Or a wayward rose to teach to twine.

Mother's sunbonnets of calico
Or checkered blue gingham made just so—
Oh, something familiar in years of old
When today was a story still untold.
But what do we know of intrinsic worth
Or dancing or plodding the ways of the earth?
Mother's sunbonnets were everyday things
With their ruffles and bows and wide tie strings.
Everyday things in my childhood years,
But in memory's annals, that which endears.

A woman reads on her way to town in David Woodlock's THE RED
BONNET. *Image from Kenulf Gallery/Fine Art Photographic Library,
London/Art Resource, New York.*

VICTORIAN HAIR JEWELRY

Laurie Hunter

A visit to my dear great-granny's house is always an enchanting step back in time. Rose water scents her bed linens; cobalt-blue glass bottles line each windowsill; and, on the bedside table, diminutive Victorian jewelry rests on folds of plush, ruby-colored satin within a gilded glass box.

At first glance, Granny's pieces are highly detailed—perfect, even. She has a bangle bracelet with a tiny crystal clasp, a pair of small hoop earrings, cuff links no bigger than dimes, and a fascinating locket-style pin depicting a mother and child. Upon closer inspection, however, startled visitors discover that each piece of jewelry is fashioned from human hair.

Many of Granny's guests with whom she has shared her collection may at first think, "What a strange thing to collect!" They are soon deeply moved, however, as they realize they are viewing rare souvenirs of a bygone era—tiny testaments to the depth of love.

For the Victorians, this type of jewelry was treasured. Each keepsake was painstakingly created by dedicated hands which were weaving strands of hair into exquisite pieces of history. A lock of hair was an intimate representation of love, joy, celebration, remembrance, and life. The jewelry, woven from strands of hair from deceased or living loved ones, was meant to be worn by generations to come. It is amazing that something crafted from material as delicate as human hair could survive for centuries and still be witnessed and appreciated today.

On my most recent visit to Granny's house, I convinced her to spend an afternoon relating the history of each piece to me. We curled up with cups of tea, delighting in her memories and creating a new one together. She fondly recalled when she acquired the bangle bracelet, the first in her collection. On her wedding day in 1926, Granny received the bracelet as a gift from her grandmother, Nana Pearl. Pearl had given a lock of her hair to her young husband as he went off to war. Upon his return, the cherished lock of hair was woven into a bracelet. Granny remembered how the bracelet had made her feel like she had many generations of her family with her for that momentous day.

Granny's eyes brimmed with tears of joy as she remembered being given the spiral hoop earrings by her husband on their fiftieth wedding anniversary. He had spotted them in a boutique on the square that sold antique jewelry gleaned from local estate sales, and he knew Granny would appreciate their intricate design.

Granny lovingly told how she was given the mother-and-child pin by a dear college friend who knew she collected Victorian jewelry. The friend's grandmother had woven it from her own hair in celebration of a much-anticipated child. The brooch with rosettes was a souvenir from a trip Granny took forty years ago with her family to the small Scandinavian town that still makes the pieces from human hair, preserving a handicraft that has all but been forgotten by the majority of the world.

It was then that I realized Granny's collection was really not so unusual. In fact, I have a lock of my own hair saved for me by my mother in a little envelope, as well as locks of my children's hair tucked into their baby books. I suppose saving a lock of hair is like taking a snapshot of a moment in time.

After returning the heirlooms to their display box, Granny paused and smiled, opened the case once more, took out the hoop earrings, and pressed them into my hand. Should I ever lose perspective on what's most important in life, she admonished, these little treasures would remind me that the best times are spent cherishing one another.

TREASURED TRESSES

If you would like to collect Victorian hair jewelry, the following information may be helpful.

A PIECE OF HISTORY

• Jewelry made of human hair dates back to at least the 1600s, when bracelets woven from hair or lockets holding human hair were sometimes given as tokens of love.

• Human hair jewelry was popularized in the nineteenth century when Queen Victoria gave a piece of jewelry made from her own hair to Empress Eugenie of France. Queen Victoria wrote in her diary that Eugenie had been "touched to tears."

• Originally, jewelry was woven from the hair of the dead and fashioned into a memento of a loved one. The trend then moved on to commemorating joyful occasions, such as births and weddings.

• The popularity of human hair jewelry began to spread to the United States during the Civil War. Loved ones would send a lock of hair with a soldier going to war. When a soldier was mortally wounded, his hair would be woven into jewelry to commemorate his life.

• Human hair ornaments maintained their popularity through the end of the nineteenth century, but the human hair jewelry craze came to an end near the onset of World War I.

• The craft of hair work is still being perpetuated in several small Scandinavian villages, such as Vamhus, Sweden, which were among the first to plait hair into jewelry.

HOME WEAVING

• In the Victorian era, weaving human hair became a homemaker's craft since the pieces were in high demand and sold at such high prices

• Housekeeping journals and books of domesticity taught women how to weave their own jewelry from hair. Printed charts and molds were also available to home weavers. Women then sent the finished pieces to a jeweler for appropriate fittings.

The basket of flowers in the brooch above is made using the hair of eight family members. Photo courtesy of Sandra Johnson, hair artist, Heritage Hair Art, Inc.

• To make a piece of jewelry, a few strands of hair were woven at a time into a plait or basket weave. The pieces were prized for their intricacy and complex design.

• Often, the plaited designs were so meticulously woven that it is difficult to recognize that the piece was made of human hair.

HAND-CRAFTED GEMS

Human hair ornaments are so detailed, they are considered by collectors to be miniature works of art. Handiworks to collect include:

• Rings	• Brooches and stick pins
• Watch chains	• Necklace pendants
• Sleeve buttons	• Hair barrettes

Scenes depicted in human hair jewelry include:

• Landscapes	• Floral designs
• Pastoral scenes	• Symbolic designs

The Old, Dear Right
Kathleen Norris

As years ago we carried to your knees
The tales and treasures of eventful days,
Knowing no deed too humble for your praise,
Nor any gift too trivial to please,
So still we bring, with older smiles and tears,
What gifts we may to claim the old, dear right;
Your faith, beyond the silence and the night,
Your love still close and watching through the years.

Tribute to a Mother
Louisa May Alcott

Faith that withstood the shocks of toil and time;
Hope that defied despair;
Patience that conquered care;
And loyalty, whose courage was sublime;
The great deep heart that was a home for all—
Just, eloquent, and strong
In protest against wrong;
Wide charity that knew no sin, no fall;
The Spartan spirit that made life so grand,
Meeting poor daily needs
With high, heroic deeds,
That wrested happiness from Fate's hard hand.

Peonies and lilacs are a fitting tribute to Mother.
Photo by D. Petku/H. Armstrong Roberts.

Her Hands

Anna Hempstead Branch

My mother's hands are cool and fair;
They can do anything.
Delicate mercies bide them there
Like flowers in the spring.

When I was small and could not sleep,
She used to come to me,
And with my cheek upon her hand
How sure my rest would be.

For everything she ever touched
Of beautiful or fine,
Their memories living in her hands
Would warm that sleep of mine.

Her hands remember how they played
One time in meadow streams,
And all the flickering song and shade
Of water took my dreams.

Swift through her haunted fingers pass
Memories of garden things;
I dipped my face in flowers and grass
And sounds of hidden wings.

One time she touched the cloud that kissed
Brown pastures bleak and far;
I leaned my cheek into a mist
And thought I was a star.

All this was very long ago
And I am grown; but yet
The hand that lured my slumber so
I never can forget.

For still when drowsiness comes on
It seems so soft and cool,
Shaped happily beneath my cheek,
Hollow and beautiful.

Mother's hands are highlighted by a bright bouquet in HANDS
WITH FLOWERS *by Bernardita Zegers. Image from Superstock.*

HANDMADE HEIRLOOM

WEDDING SAMPLERS

Melissa Lester

When I am reflecting on life's transitions, sometimes needlework can express for me what words alone cannot. I share my love of needlework with my husband's Aunt Carla, who is particularly interested in wedding samplers. Her creativity has blessed many newly-weds with a cherished keepsake.

Carla's interest in samplers was fueled by a rare find she stumbled upon several years ago. While her husband researched genealogy at a vast college library, she strolled the halls. As she admired artwork on the walls, she was stunned to find a sampler stitched by one of her ancestors. Instantly she felt a connection to the young girl who worked the sampler in the 1800s. Carla, excited by the discovery, sketched a copy of the piece to take home. The resulting sampler she stitched includes her own name and family history and is a treasured heirloom.

Wedding samplers became popular in the nineteenth century, but history has been documented in samplers for centuries. In Europe, early samplers were long, narrow band samplers intended to serve as the needlewoman's workbook for practicing and recording stitches used in costume decoration. The samplers could then be used as a reference tool to reproduce designs.

By the seventeenth century, printed pattern books were being circulated, so samplers lost some of their value as works of reference. Children were working samplers by this time. At their mothers' urging, young girls practiced techniques and learned new borders. Needlework was a serious exercise, and the quality of a student's workmanship was thought to reflect the skill of the instructor.

Although the craft was very popular in England, needlework was a luxury few early American settlers could afford. The ornate forms of needlework were not economically beneficial, and life was simply too difficult for leisurely pursuits. Although some of the colonial women probably brought a few precious materials with them to the new land, they had no way to replenish their supplies until sheep were brought from Europe. Then embroidery wool could be made that rivaled the wool used in England.

By the mid-eighteenth century, needlework was considered a major part of a young girl's education on both sides of the ocean. Girls worked samplers in the form most recognized today: letters

> *Each wedding sampler unfolds as a beautiful representation of its intended recipients.*

and numbers arranged symmetrically, balanced by decorative elements, and framed by a border. Common motifs included animals, flowers, and houses. Samplers from this time also included religious verses, geography, and even mathematics.

During Victorian times, samplers became more decorative than educational. Though pictorial designs became more complicated, the number of stitches employed decreased. One stitch that endured is the cross-stitch that is popular today.

In the nineteenth century, samplers became a popular way to create family registers. A common design for wedding samplers featured a center block of text with columns on each side and an arch above decorated with floral wreaths. On other designs, family names were stitched onto the fruit of a genealogical tree. Wedding and birth samplers from this period are heirlooms treasured by many families, whereas collectors value them for their social history.

By the end of the nineteenth century, interest in making samplers had waned. It seemed then as if the door had closed on this centuries-old art, but the end of the twentieth century brought a resurgence of interest in the craft. New technology has made the supply of fabric and thread colors nearly limitless. And now with computers, the modern needleworker can design, personalize, and adapt sampler patterns before the first stitch is sewn. Reproduction patterns allow needleworkers to duplicate samplers stitched long ago.

Aunt Carla draws inspiration from Dutch samplers of the Victorian era. She chooses motifs for her wedding samplers with religious symbolism that is unique to the Dutch, perhaps including a crown to represent the voice of God or a dove to signify God's words. For the bride, she might include a pink carnation for motherhood; for the groom, a duck for fidelity. Each sampler unfolds as a beautiful representation of its intended recipients, with designs and colors planned to reflect each couple's personality and tastes.

With her plan in mind, Carla often chooses perforated paper to work her sampler. She enjoys working with the sturdy paper, which she says many needleworkers favored during Victorian times because it was less expensive than linen. She stitches each sampler with wool floss, often working beads or metallic thread into the design, and frames the finished piece in an antique frame. Carla begins each project with love and good wishes in her heart for the recipient and finishes by stitching her name and the date.

With the demands of raising two young boys, I have difficulty finding the time or solitude for needlework these days. But years from now, perhaps I will sit down with Aunt Carla to plan wedding samplers for my grown sons. As we explore books of centuries-old designs, Carla and I will look for the perfect motifs to represent each groom and his chosen bride. And as I prepare to face that transition with needle in hand, with each stitch will come a prayer of hope for a lifetime of wedded bliss.

Many hours and good wishes are stitched into this wedding sampler designed by Teresa Wentzler. Photo compliments of Leisure Arts, Inc., U.S.A.

A Wedding Gift

Grace V. Watkins

I wish you more than merely happiness,
For happiness will be a fragile thing
To shelter you in rain and storm unless
Your hearts possess a stronger covering.
So I would wish you hope and faith and all
The deep sustaining wonderment of prayer.
And if within some darkened hour, a tall
Forbidding mountain hides the rising star,
Oh, climb together, climb the rugged hill;
And you will see the starlight shining still.

On Our Daughter's Wedding Day

Wesley H. Hager

Dear Father, for this day of dreams,
This holy, sacred hour,
We give Thee thanks and praise Thy name
For love that's come to flower.

For kneeling at Thy altar now,
Two hearts that beat as one,
Our daughter and the man she loves,
Their new life now begun.

A quarter century ago
We knelt where now they kneel;
We dreamed the selfsame dreams they dream
And felt what now they feel.

For us the long years seem so short;
Forgive our too-moist eyes.
For them the short years dragged along,
This day's sun slow to rise.

Give them joy, success, and laughter,
Mingled with life's work and tears,
Make their home a place of peace where
Love keeps growing through the years.

A festive table, complete with tiny lambs, is set for the wedding party. Photo by Jessie Walker.

To My Other Mother

Judy Nilson

You are the mother I received
The day I wed your son,
And I just want to thank you, Mom,
For loving things you've done.

You've given me a gracious man
With whom I share my life.
You are his lovely mother,
And I, his lucky wife.

You used to pat his little head,
And now I hold his hand.
You raised in love a little boy
And then gave me the man.

To My Mother-in-Law

Nancy Lee Beggin

You never dried my tears
When I was a little girl.
You never planned my future
With each homemade curl.

Your arms didn't await me
When my school day was done.
You didn't share my triumphs
Or my childhood fun.

But you are a mother
Who bore a child
And molded his manhood
On which God smiled.

And then love reached out,
Encompassing my heart,
And brought to love's altar
A new life to start.

A miracle of birth,
Binding our love for all to see—
Your son, my husband,
Our children, your immortality.

So today, Mother dear,
Mine through deepest love,
May the God who gave you life
Bless and guide you from above.

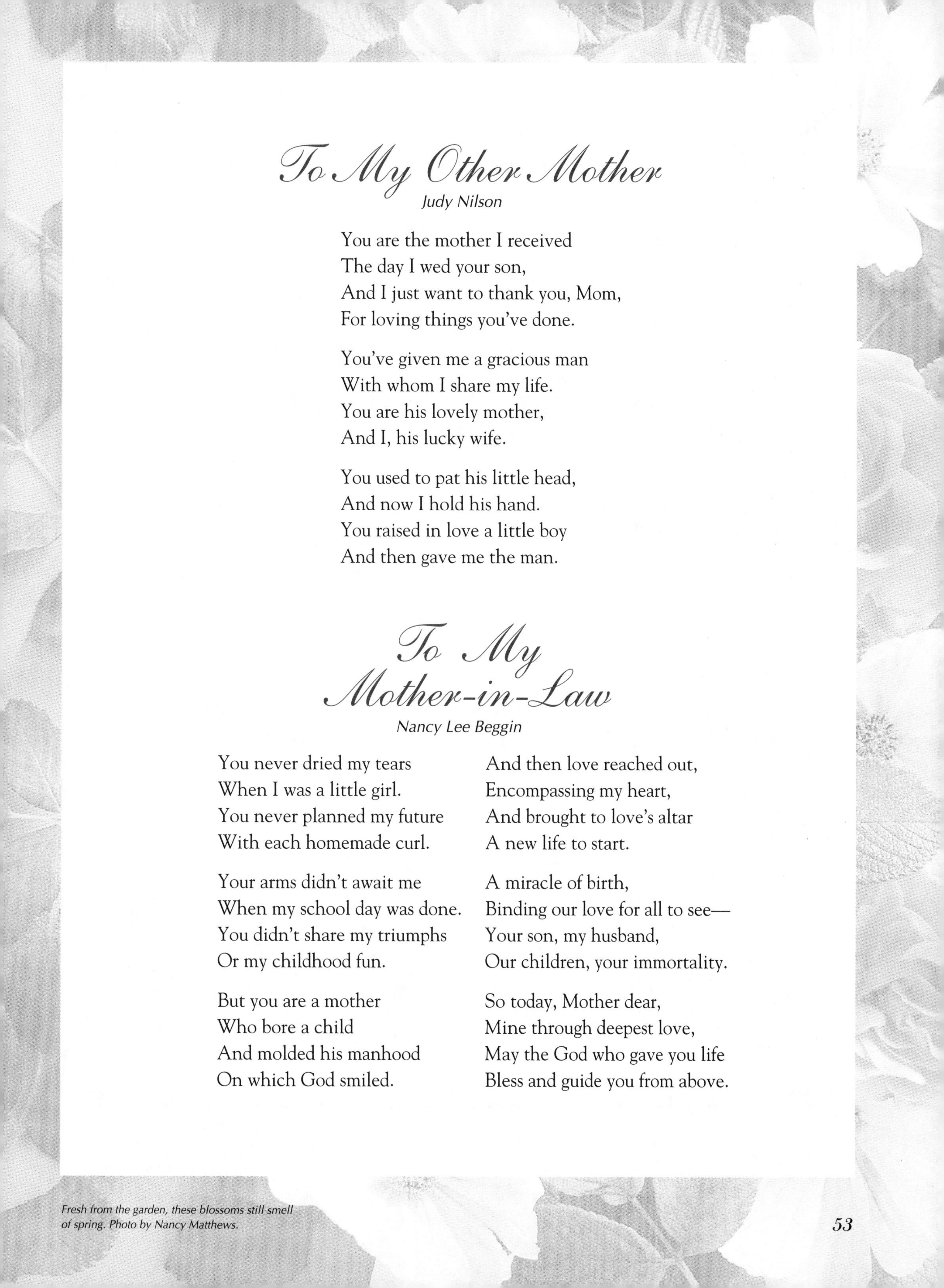

Fresh from the garden, these blossoms still smell of spring. Photo by Nancy Matthews.

I drank in, as a plant from the soil, the first nourishing juices of my young intellect from the books carefully selected by my mother. But I drank deep, above all, from my mother's mind. —Alphonse de Lamartine

The Reading Mother

Strickland Gillilan

I had a mother who read to me
Sagas of pirates who scoured the sea,
Cutlasses clenched in their yellow teeth,
"Blackbirds" stowed in the hold beneath.

I had a mother who read me lays
Of ancient and gallant and golden days,
Stories of Marmion and Ivanhoe
Which every boy has a right to know.

I had a mother who read me tales
Of Gêlert the hound of the hills of Wales,

True to his trust till his tragic death,
Faithfulness blent with his final breath.

I had a mother who read me the things
That wholesome life to the boy-heart brings—
Stories that stir with an upward touch.
Oh, that each mother of boys were such!

You may have tangible wealth untold,
Caskets of jewels and coffers of gold.
Richer than I you can never be—
I had a mother who read to me.

Judicious mothers will always keep in mind that they are the first book read and the last put aside in every child's library. —C. Lenox Remond

LEGENDARY Americans

HARRIET BEECHER STOWE

Peggy Schaefer

During the early nineteenth century, American society valued women less than men; revered preachers as moral and social leaders; and accepted the practice of slavery, actively in the South and passively in the North. Into this environment came Harriet Beecher Stowe, the daughter of a Calvinist preacher in New England—a woman who was reportedly welcomed into the world by her father with the words, "Wisht it had been a boy." Who could have known that she would write a novel that would prompt Abraham Lincoln, upon meeting her, to declare, "So this is the little lady who started this big war"?

A COUNTRY DIVIDED

At the time of Harriet's birth in Litchfield, Connecticut, on June 14, 1811, the issue of slavery in the United States had not yet become divisive. The North frowned upon slavery, but the South considered it to be economically necessary. The Missouri Compromise of 1820 was expected to preserve the balance between slave and free states, but the Compromise proved inadequate, and conflict between the North and South grew.

A FAMILY OF PREACHERS

The sixth of eight siblings and three stepsiblings, young Harriet, or "Hattie" as she was called, was an intelligent and shy child. Early on, she sought refuge from the noise and clamor of her big family in the pages of books. Lyman Beecher, Harriet's

larger-than-life father, was perhaps New England's best known preacher, and all of her brothers eventually became preachers as well.

Harriet's oldest sister Catharine opened a succession of girls' schools in the cities in which the family lived, and Harriet was drawn into her employ as a teacher at the age of fourteen. While teaching at Catharine's Hartford Female Academy, Harriet had a room of her own for the first time, and she used this opportunity to develop her interest in writing.

In 1832, the Beecher family moved to Cincinnati, at the time a booming river city geographically at the center of the slavery debate. There Harriet discovered the tragic impact of the slave trade. She met free blacks and escaped slaves, heard stories of the Underground Railroad, and saw posters advertising the sale of slaves. The Beecher family strongly opposed slavery but felt the abolitionist movement was too extreme a measure. Their beliefs, along with those of other Northerners, were soon to change.

NAME: Harriet Beecher Stowe

BORN: June 14, 1811, Litchfield, Connecticut

MARRIED: Calvin Stowe

CHILDREN: Twins Harriet and Eliza, Henry, Frederick, Georgianna, Charles Edward (Samuel Charles died at the age of eighteen months.)

ACCOMPLISHMENTS: *Uncle Tom's Cabin* sold more than 300,000 copies in its first year

NOVELS: *Uncle Tom's Cabin; Dred; The Minister's Wooing; The Pearl of Orr's Island; Oldtown Folks*

QUOTE: "What man has nerve to do, man has not nerve to hear."

A Writer Grows

While in Cincinnati, Harriet published her first book, a geography book for children, although the publisher insisted on listing Catharine as co-author. Harriet became a charter member of the Semi-Colon Club and developed her gift for bringing familiar characters to life and for incorporating the stories of those she knew into her writing.

In 1836 Harriet married Calvin Stowe, the widower of her friend Eliza Stowe and a member of the faculty at Lane Theological Seminary. The Panic of 1837 brought financial hardships to the Stowes, and Harriet turned to writing to supplement her husband's salary.

Change Brings Action

With the passage of the Compromise of 1850, Congress hoped to calm the growing conflict between North and South by allowing new territories to decide for themselves whether to allow slavery. Most troubling to Northerners was the Fugitive Slave Act, which required those in the North to return escaped slaves to their owners.

The Beecher family became increasingly vocal, with the men using their pulpits to speak out against slavery. Harriet's sister-in-law Isabella was particularly incensed and wrote to her: "Hattie, if I could use a pen as you can, I would write something that would make this whole nation feel what an accursed thing slavery is." Harriet was busy with the challenges of raising children and managing the Stowes' strained finances. But Isabella's words motivated her, and she exclaimed, "God, helping me, I will write something. I will if I live."

While in church one Sunday, Harriet had a vision of a slave of dignity and great faith being beaten to death by two other slaves while their master watched. She put pen to paper, and the words that poured out became the climax of her novel. Harriet negotiated a fee of three hundred dollars for a three- to four-installment serial, and

Harriet Beecher Stowe. Image from H. Armstrong Roberts.

Uncle Tom's Cabin, an antislavery novel that rocked the country, was born.

When published in book form in 1852, *Uncle Tom's Cabin* sold more than 300,000 copies in its first year and brought the issue of slavery to the forefront of American society. The book was translated into foreign languages and adapted for the stage. It was in later dramatizations of the novel, "Tom shows," that "Uncle Tom" came to be construed as an insult, meaning a foolish person overly eager to please—unfortunately a characterization far from Harriet's original depiction.

Harriet Beecher Stowe went on to write for more than twenty years, both novels and articles for newspapers and magazines. She will always be remembered best for her antislavery novel that focused the world's attention on a grave injustice and helped to bring an end to slavery. She died in 1896 at the age of eighty-five.

My Dear, Dear Georgiana,

Only think how long it is since I have written to you, and how changed I am since then—the mother of three children! Well, if I have not kept the reckoning of old times, let this last circumstance prove my apology, for I have been hand, heart, and head full since I saw you.

Now, today, for example, I'll tell you what I had on my mind from dawn to dewy eve. In the first place I waked about half after four and thought, "Bless me, how light it is! I must get out of bed and rap to wake up Mina, for breakfast must be had at six o'clock this morning." So out of bed I jump and seize the tongs and pound, pound, pound over poor Mina's sleepy head, charitably allowing her about half an hour to get waked up in,—that being the quantum of time that it takes me,— or used to.

Well, then baby wakes, "Qua, qua, qua," so I give him his breakfast. I get my frock half on and baby by that time has kicked himself down off his pillow, and is crying and fisting the bedclothes in great order. I stop with one sleeve off and one on to settle matters with him. Having planted him bolt upright and gone all up and down the chamber barefoot to get pillows and blankets to prop him up, I finish putting my frock on and hurry down to satisfy myself by actual observation that the breakfast is in progress. Then back I come into the nursery, where, remembering that it is washing day and that there is a great deal of work to be done, I apply myself vigorously to sweeping, dusting, and the setting to rights so necessary where there are three little mischiefs always pulling down as fast as one can put up.

Then there are Miss H[attie] and Miss E[liza], concerning whom Mary [Beecher Perkins] will furnish you with all suitable particulars, who are chattering, hallooing, or singing at the tops of their voices, as may suit their various states of mind, while the nurse is getting their breakfast ready.

This meal being cleared away, Mr. Stowe dispatched to market with various memoranda of provisions, etc., and the baby being washed and dressed, I begin to think what next must be done. I start to cut out some little dresses, have just calculated the length and got one breadth torn off when Master Henry makes a doleful lip and falls to crying with might and main. I catch him up and turning round see one of his sisters flourishing the things out of my workbox in fine style.

Moving it away and looking the other side I see the second little mischief seated by the hearth chewing coals and scraping up ashes with great apparent relish. Grandmother lays hold upon her and charitably offers to endeavor to quiet baby while I go on with my work. I set at it again, pick up a dozen pieces, measure them once more to see which is the right one, and proceed to cut out some others, when I see the twins on the point of quarreling with each other. Number one pushes number two over. Number two screams: that frightens the baby and he joins in. I call number one a naughty girl, take the persecuted one in my arms, and endeavor to comfort her.

Meanwhile number one makes her way to the

Sisters enjoy a game of peekaboo in Children Playing *by Erik Theodor Werenskiold. Image from Christie's Images.*

slop jar and forthwith proceeds to wash her apron in it. Grandmother catches her by one shoulder, drags her away, and sets the jar out of her reach. By and by the nurse comes up from her sweeping. I commit the children to her, and finish cutting out the frocks.

But let this suffice, for of such details as these are all my days made up. Indeed, my dear, I am but a mere drudge with few ideas beyond babies and housekeeping. As for thoughts, reflections, and sentiments, good lack! good lack!

I suppose I am a dolefully uninteresting person at present, but I hope I shall grow young again one of these days, for it seems to me that matters cannot always stand exactly as they do now.

Well, Georgy, this marriage is—yes, I will speak well of it, after all; for when I can stop and think long enough to discriminate my head from my heels, I must say that I think myself a fortunate woman both in husband and children. My children I would not change for all the ease, leisure, and pleasure that I could have without them. They are money on interest whose value will be constantly increasing.

Harriet

Letter from Harriet Beecher Stowe to her friend Georgiana May Sykes, June 21, 1838

The Harriet Beecher Stowe Center

Hartford, Connecticut

D. Fran Morley

Most people know Harriet Beecher Stowe as the author of *Uncle Tom's Cabin*, one of the most influential works in American literature. However, as I learned on a recent visit to the Harriet Beecher Stowe Center in Hartford, Connecticut, Mrs. Stowe accomplished much more than writing just this one book.

Mrs. Stowe wrote thirty books and hundreds of articles on almost every subject, from religion to household hints. As a supportive wife and mother of seven children, she wrote out of financial necessity. She also had an intense personal drive to help right society's wrongs; with her pen, she managed to change the world. Today, the Stowe Center presents a historical representation of her life, but it is also a research center that continues Mrs. Stowe's important work.

In the midst of busy Hartford, the Stowe Center is part of historic Nook Farm, now a mixed-use neighborhood with only a few remaining Victorian homes. But Nook Farm was once a thriving community of intellectuals, writers, and social activists who enjoyed each other's company. The Stowe Center includes the seventeen-room Victorian brick home to which Harriet and Calvin Stowe retired in 1873; eight fully restored gardens; the Stowe Center Library; a carriage house that now serves as visitor center and museum gift shop; and the Katharine Seymour Day House, once

home to Mrs. Stowe's grandniece, who was instrumental in saving the historic neighborhood and laying the foundations for the Stowe Center.

As I walked onto the tranquil grounds of the Stowe Center, I felt swept back in time. I stopped by the visitor center to look over exhibits and the gift shop, then caught up with a tour entering the Stowe home. Our guide, a student from nearby Hartford High School, explained that the Stowes were "downsizing" when they moved into this home that had been built two years earlier for a Hartford attorney. At five thousand square feet, the home was substantial but small for its time in Nook Farm. The three-story brick home, recently

---

The making of bright, happy homes is the best way of helping on the world that has been discovered yet.—H. B. Stowe

---

painted in a historically accurate dove gray, is referred to as a cottage because of its steeply pitched roof. Modest gingerbread trim outlines the eaves, and the windows are trimmed with shutters in a slightly darker gray.

Inside, the home has a warm, comfortable feel that reflects Mrs. Stowe's homemaking philosophy. Much of the home is exactly as she arranged it, thanks to detailed descriptions in letters written to her adult daughters.

Oddly enough, Mrs. Stowe did not describe her kitchen, but our guide noted that it was designed according to *American Woman's Home*, an 1869 book written by Mrs. Stowe and her sister, Catharine Beecher. I was impressed with the kitchen's efficient layout, handy bins, and convenient work areas. Two taps at the kitchen sink weren't for hot and cold water, as I imagined. The practical Mrs. Stowe had one tap to draw city water

Harriet Beecher Stowe's home is a testament to Victorian life. Photo courtesy the Harriet Beecher Stowe Center.

space, it is easy to imagine Mrs. Stowe returning to her desk by the window, taking up her quill pen, and resuming her work.

My tour continued with a walk through the Katharine Seymour Day House. Much of this magnificent Queen Anne style mansion is now used for administrative purposes, but it also contains the library reading room as well as program and exhibit space. I enjoyed seeing many of Mrs. Stowe's other writings, foreign translations of *Uncle Tom's Cabin*, and a priceless letter from a ten-year-old

for cooking and drinking and another to draw water from the cistern for washing.

We toured the formal front parlor where Mrs. Stowe entertained her many distinguished guests from around the world. The rear parlor was for family, and its comfortable furnishings reflect this use. Like all the rooms, these have a mix of eighteenth- and nineteenth-century pieces, as well as artwork and memorabilia collected by the Stowes during their lecture tours in Europe to discuss *Uncle Tom's Cabin*.

The second floor family bedrooms, including Mrs. Stowe's sitting room, are comfortable, with simple furnishings and items picked up in their travels. Several landscapes painted by Mrs. Stowe decorate the rooms.

Mrs. Stowe's bedroom is a sunny, bright room. A large terrarium filled with native ferns and mosses rests near the bay window, and trailing vines climb around the window to the ceiling. An avid gardener, Mrs. Stowe preferred live plants to heavy window coverings. In such an intimate

Harriet to her big brother, Edward. In addition to the historic pieces, it was interesting to review material from current programs that allow students and teachers to continue to benefit from Mrs. Stowe's inspiration. I vowed to return another time to take full advantage of the research library. With more than 180,000 manuscripts, twelve thousand images, and twelve thousand books, it is open to the public by appointment.

On my way out, I lingered in the gardens, enjoying the pink dogwood tree that dates from Mrs. Stowe's lifetime. An effort to propagate the tree has been most successful, and saplings have now been planted in Cincinnati, Japan, and Canada.

As I made my passage back to the twenty-first century, I realized how significant it is that this is called the Harriet Beecher Stowe Center. While it does historically preserve Mrs. Stowe's home and surroundings, the facility also serves the future, and it continues Mrs. Stowe's work to inspire social justice for all.

Two Grandmothers

Inga Gilson Caldwell

They talk of life as they had lived it when,
Some sixty years ago, they both were young;
Bright little memories, like golden beads
Upon the frailest silver necklace strung.

Each memory revives some incident
Of early married life, of hardships shared,
Of children gathered round, of work and play,
Of little broken hopes by love repaired.

I see the picture which they paint; brushed
With shaky hands upon time's canvas, spread
For two grandmothers who are busily,
With shining shuttle, weaving memories' thread.

Rebound

Johnielu Barber Bradford

My grandmother told me stories when I was small—
True stories of plantation childhood days.
Oh, that was long ago; still I recall
The lessons taught in kind, inspiring ways.
"Once upon a time," began her story,
And she would talk through smiles, and sometimes tears.
And always I would thrill to share the glory
Of one I counted great through all her years.
"Once upon a time"—four words to start
A happy glow in young admiring eyes—
The light love kindles in a child's true heart.
No critic would approve, I realize;
Yet how I long to start each sonnet of mine
With that delightful "Once upon a time."

THE BUTTON BOX

Vivian Conrad

I hadn't thought about it until my son, Joshua, popped a button. We scurried about the house looking for another one to replace it. We dug through my sewing cabinet, closet shelves, and kitchen junk drawer. We even sifted through my costume jewelry and my husband's tools. But among the handful of odd buttons we uncovered, there was not one the size or color we needed for Joshua's shirt.

For the first time in my adult life, it struck me that I didn't have a button box. Generations of sensible American housewives had kept one. My mother's was a red fruitcake tin with a Currier and Ives print on the lid.

Mom's button box was a source of continual amusement during my childhood. It contained buttons of myriad sizes, shapes, and colors. I remember spending long afternoons digging and sorting, delighting in the uniqueness of some buttons and the uniformity of others. Some were large and round, made of shimmering mother-of-pearl. Others were studded with rhinestones or decorated with tiny, delicately carved flowers. The small, white shirt buttons seemed identical, as did the larger plastic buttons that were just the right size for closing skirt bands and trousers. I found buttons with rough or smooth textures and geometric shapes, as well as those with irregular surface patterns and unusual designs. A few bespoke sleek elegance, while another whimsical lot had originally adorned children's clothes. Red disks, pink ones, yellow and lavender, blue and brown—a treasure pile of buttons for busy little hands.

But even more appealing than the colors and textures in the box were the stories connected with various buttons. Time and again I'd carry an unusual find to my mother and ask "Where did this come from?" As she turned the button over in her hand, a faint smile would tug at the corners of her mouth. Her eyes glowed with a distant light as she remembered people and places from long ago and far away.

"This button came from your Great-Aunt Mary's gray coat. I remember the time . . ." And off we would fly on an adventure with Aunt Mary, or Grandfather Holland, or whomever had first worn the button. The box contained pieces of my

> *I remember spending long afternoons digging and sorting through my mother's button box.*

heritage, and I considered it an integral part of my family tree.

As I grew up and started a home of my own, I somehow forgot about the button box. I did not sew for my children as my mother had for me. It was too easy to catch clearance sales at discount stores. And if someone lost a button, I often just ran to the drugstore at the end of the block for a quick replacement.

My preschoolers passed their days playing with blocks and modeling clay and watching children's shows on television. They entered kindergarten and progressed to letters and numbers. My husband and I bought educational toys and supplied enrichment tools to encourage the children's love of learning. As they matured, they learned to appreciate the resource books they used to locate facts and figures for school projects. But the day Joshua lost his shirt button, I suddenly began to take a new look around my home.

What memorabilia did I have that my children associated with their heritage? What knickknacks sitting around the house would prompt questions about their past, about people and places that were important links to our family history? Had I ever taken time to acquaint them with relatives who dated beyond my parents' generation?

I realized that my children had never heard the story of Great-Aunt Mary's gray coat. I had somehow neglected to pass along the tale of Great-Aunt Madeline, who as a child had jumped off the pumphouse roof and landed on a chicken. My sons and daughters didn't know that their great-grandfather had lost his first wife and child in an influenza epidemic during World War I or that my great-grandfather had been a circuit-riding preacher in the Old South. No one had told them that Great-Uncle Jack's father led a notorious band of raiders during the Civil War. Were they aware that my father's dad was a lawyer and state senator before

he became a church pastor? My children were losing touch with their roots, and I felt responsible.

My generation may be technologically sophisticated, but we still need our button boxes. I want my children to learn about their ancestors,

> Time and again I'd carry an unusual find to my mother and ask "Where did this come from?"

to say of certain stories or events, "This is what shaped us and helped make us what we are. This is who I am."

It may be difficult to find time for stories during today's hectic schedules, but I am determined to set aside moments to gather my children around the open button box and retell tales and remember people and places from long ago and far away. I owe them their heritage.

A menagerie of buttons waits to be discovered by little hands. Photo by Dianne Dietrich Leis.

Grandma's Playthings

Ruth Selden White

When we children went to
    Grandma's house,
We climbed up the back stair
Into a little attic room.
She kept the playthings there.
Tommy rode the rocking horse;
He liked that best of all.
I liked the wicker carriage
And Grandma's black-eyed doll.
Upon a shelf in the corner
Sat her teddy bear;
She'd hugged this favorite pet so
She'd rubbed off most of his hair.
A picture hung upon the wall
Of her as she used to be,
And Mama used to smile and say
How much it looked like me.

Young girls share an afternoon of discovery in
GRANDMA'S TREASURES *by artist Kathryn Andrews*
Fincher. Image courtesy of the artist.

Grandmother's Doll

Peggy Mlcuch

For years you've lain in Grandma's trunk
Among those things she held most dear—
Her wedding dress, some baby shoes,
Some lovely bits of yesteryear;
A lock of hair, a book of poems,
Some letters gently tied in blue;
A lacy fan, a valentine,
Some flowers that she'd pressed, and you.

I Look Just Like Her

Danielle Aiello

When I was little,
I'd go up in my grandmother's bathroom
And watch my mother and grandmother, down
In the kitchen, through a hole in the floor.

Over the clanging of pots and pans,
I heard their laughter,
Saw their connection,
And loved every minute they spent together.

When I was younger,
My mother and I could fit
In our chair together perfectly.
I couldn't drift off into dreamland
Without her kiss good night.

All my friends say I look just like her.
When I get older,
I hope to see my mother in my daughter's eyes.

Love to a Grandmother

Hal Moore

Sometimes in a half-hidden, misty way,
In the eyes of my little girl,
I can see the spark of my mother's eyes.
Curious how that spark can rise
In the eyes of a little girl.

Again, in a dim, foreshortened way,
In the face of my little girl,
I can see the curve of my mother's chin
And the jaunty twist of my mother's grin
In the face of my little girl.

I hope, as the years meander by,
And time takes its toll on us,
That like Mother's eyes and Mother's face
I'll see Mother's charm and Mother's grace
In the face of my little girl.

An elaborate vanity gathers all of Grandmother's favorite things. Photo by Jessie Walker.

Once Again

Craig E. Sathoff

Before we knew, the years had flown,
And all our kids were gone from home.
The days seemed long and lonely then,
Until we had our grandchildren.

And so it seems a special treat
With children once more round our feet,
For once again the youngsters are
Raiding Grandma's cookie jar.

The tire swing is back in play,
And cowboys romp by on their way
In search of bandits fast and bold
Who have a wealth of hidden gold.

We've picnics in the woods nearby
And paper airplanes made to fly.
We've fishing trips and bats and balls
And wiener roasts in lovely fall.

The world seems such a splendid place,
Made precious by each smiling face,
Each little hand, each fond hello
That grandparents treasure so.

A little boy steals his first picnic kiss.
Photo by Dianne Dietrich Leis.

Pamela Kennedy

"Therefore do not worry about tomorrow, for tomorrow will worry about itself. Each day has enough trouble of its own." Matthew 6:34 (NIV)

WORRIED MOTHERS

I am so worried about my son. You know if he gets a poor grade he may never get into his first choice of colleges." "I can't believe she's three and still isn't toilet trained. Do you think there's something wrong?" "Will he make friends?" "Will she be safe?" "What if he never marries?" "Do you think they'll ever have kids?"

If you're a mother or a grandmother, chances are, thoughts like these have run through your head. Perhaps some even set up housekeeping there. Mothers seem to make careers out of worrying about their children. From the time they're born until long after they're grown, we just can't seem to stop fretting about them. Worries and concerns flood our daytime thoughts and sometimes even keep us awake at night. Yet researchers tell us that worrying accomplishes little besides creating more worries. Recently I read the following: "Many of our worries are about things that have already happened and, therefore, can't be changed. Even more of our worries are about the future, and things that may never actually happen. That leaves only a tiny percentage of our worries about things happening right now—and most of those are beyond our control." The author concluded that worry is the ultimate waste of time. My grandmother didn't have a degree in psychology, but she came to the same conclusion: "Worry is

like rocking in a chair; it takes up time and energy, but it gets you nowhere." Why then, do so many of us worry?

A clue can be found in Matthew 6:25–34 as Jesus describes three reasons people worry. We worry because we lack faith, because we lose focus, and because we have confused priorities. I think each of these offers a key that might help us lock worry out of our lives.

When we worry, we are telling God we don't think He can take care of us; yet Jesus says that all around us in nature we see examples of His abundant provision. Animals and plants are beautifully clothed and adequately fed. God cares for them, and He will provide for us as well. The first key is to trust Him.

When we fret and stew over things that are temporal, we reveal that we value the things of this world more than the kingdom of God. Yet He gen-

> Heavenly Father, thank You for Your loving provision. Change my worry to wonder as I trust in You day by day. Amen.

tly reminds us that if we will cease our worry and seek after that which is eternal—peace, righteousness, love, truth—we will find true satisfaction. And, as an added blessing, He will provide those temporal needs as well. The second key is to change our focus.

Worry about tomorrow takes our eyes off of what is important today. There are tasks that can only be accomplished today, needs that can only be met today, people who long for love today. When we are anxious about tomorrow, we miss present opportunities. Jesus reminds His followers, "each day has enough trouble of its own." Taking care of the present trouble may even prevent those things we worry about from happening

Devotions FROM THE Heart

Pamela Kennedy

"Therefore do not worry about tomorrow, for tomorrow will worry about itself. Each day has enough trouble of its own." Matthew 6:34 (NIV)

WORRIED MOTHERS

I am so worried about my son. You know if he gets a poor grade he may never get into his first choice of colleges." "I can't believe she's three and still isn't toilet trained. Do you think there's something wrong?" "Will he make friends?" "Will she be safe?" "What if he never marries?" "Do you think they'll ever have kids?"

If you're a mother or a grandmother, chances are, thoughts like these have run through your head. Perhaps some even set up housekeeping there. Mothers seem to make careers out of worrying about their children. From the time they're born until long after they're grown, we just can't seem to stop fretting about them. Worries and concerns flood our daytime thoughts and sometimes even keep us awake at night. Yet researchers tell us that worrying accomplishes little besides creating more worries. Recently I read the following: "Many of our worries are about things that have already happened and, therefore, can't be changed. Even more of our worries are about the future, and things that may never actually happen. That leaves only a tiny percentage of our worries about things happening right now—and most of those are beyond our control." The author concluded that worry is the ultimate waste of time. My grandmother didn't have a degree in psychology, but she came to the same conclusion: "Worry is

like rocking in a chair; it takes up time and energy, but it gets you nowhere." Why then, do so many of us worry?

A clue can be found in Matthew 6:25–34 as Jesus describes three reasons people worry. We worry because we lack faith, because we lose focus, and because we have confused priorities. I think each of these offers a key that might help us lock worry out of our lives.

When we worry, we are telling God we don't think He can take care of us; yet Jesus says that all around us in nature we see examples of His abundant provision. Animals and plants are beautifully clothed and adequately fed. God cares for them, and He will provide for us as well. The first key is to trust Him.

When we fret and stew over things that are temporal, we reveal that we value the things of this world more than the kingdom of God. Yet He gen-

> Heavenly Father, thank You for Your loving provision. Change my worry to wonder as I trust in You day by day. Amen.

tly reminds us that if we will cease our worry and seek after that which is eternal—peace, righteousness, love, truth—we will find true satisfaction. And, as an added blessing, He will provide those temporal needs as well. The second key is to change our focus.

Worry about tomorrow takes our eyes off of what is important today. There are tasks that can only be accomplished today, needs that can only be met today, people who long for love today. When we are anxious about tomorrow, we miss present opportunities. Jesus reminds His followers, "each day has enough trouble of its own." Taking care of the present trouble may even prevent those things we worry about from happening

A concerned mother comforts her child in MOTHER WITH LEFT HAND HOLDING SARA'S CHIN *by artist Mary Cassatt. Image from Christie's Images.*

in the future. The third key is to choose to do the things we can today.

As mothers and grandmothers, we have the great privilege of influencing young lives. It can be an overwhelming responsibility at times, yet worrying will only sap our strength and set a poor example. If we have the courage to trust in God, to keep our eyes focused upon His priorities, and to prayerfully meet the challenges of each day, we just may produce sons and daughters of faith and confidence—children who understand the futility of worry.

OUT OF THE PAST, LILACS

Edna Greene Hines

The eternal perfume of the lilacs
Has entered my soul and become a part
Of it. Subtle, mysterious, hauntingly sweet;
I would bathe in this pool of fragrance
In the dewy dawn of the morning,
In the cool of the evening, or wet
With the damp of a gentle rain.
Out of the past I have lived with it,
Out of the days and years gone by when
Every May brought its recurring loveliness.
Out of these blessed memories of lilac beauty,
The beloved flowers of old homesteads and loves,
Supreme it reigns, the wonder-gift of May.

A FAR-OFF REASON

Isla Paschal Richardson

In every yard where children play,
Lilacs should grow.
When purple clustered blossoms sway
And soft winds blow,
Some future time, far, far away,
Their thoughts will go
Back to some happy childhood day.
Then they will know
Why in each yard where children play
Lilacs should grow.

Lilac blossoms tumble over a wooden fence in Martha's Vineyard, Massachusetts. Photo by Dick Dietrich.

Things They'll Remember

Edna Jaques

When they are old, these are the sort of things
They will remember as the years go by,
A little gilt-edged card with roses on,
A fleece of carded clouds against the sky.

They will remember cookies warm and good,
The taste of apples from a sun-warmed tree,
The feel of earth against their naked feet,
The thrill of seeing ships put out to sea.

A dress she loved, a treasured pair of shoes,
A doll that spoke, a little rocking chair,
A birthday cake with silver candles on,
The fearful shadows falling on the stair.

A boy will treasure in his deepest heart
The memory of the dog who worshipped him,
The swimmin' hole, cool water on his feet,
The shadows in a forest cool and dim.

They will remember, as the years go by,
Dreams lovely as the day, hope's shining wings,
Like incense for their soul's eternal peace,
The lovely comfort of remembered things.

The heart hath its own memory,
*   like the mind,*
And in it are enshrined
The precious keepsakes
*   into which is wrought*
The giver's loving thought.
*   —Henry Wadsworth Longfellow*

Azaleas are reflected in a pond at South Carolina's Magnolia Plantation.
Photo by Daniel E. Dempster.

FOR THE CHILDREN

Tommy

Gwendolyn Brooks

I put a seed into the ground
And said, "I'll watch it grow."
I watered it and cared for it
As well as I could know.

One day I walked in my backyard,
And oh, what did I see!
My seed had popped itself right out
Without consulting me.

A young gardener tends to her flowers in Nantucket Gardener, *an original oil painting by Donald Zolan. Copyright © Zolan Fine Arts, LLC, Ridgefield, Connecticut. All rights reserved.*

If You Grow a Garden

Helen Loomis Linham

There are many who would call me poor—
'Tis true indeed, and yet it is not so.
My cottage is a small one; at my door
Are honeysuckle vines and golden glow.
My windows hold petunias, pink and red;
And on my mantel, paper rosebuds bloom.
Indeed my soul with beauty, too, is fed,
For we have flowers in most every room.
And I have such a lovely garden now,
With cosmos growing very pink and tall.
And I have graceful four-o'clocks. Somehow,
I do not feel that I am poor at all.
For if you grow a garden, oh, I'm sure,
You never, never can be very poor.

A bench waits along a shady garden trail in Missouri. Photo by Gay Bumgarner.

Lansing Christman

COUNTRY WALKS

I take my country walks for the peace and comfort that may be found in the soothing arms of the hills. On these journeys afield, I never hurry. There are no time limits, no goals; I walk until I am satisfied. These meandering excursions give me the privilege of admiring the beauty of the flowers along the way and of hearing the songs of birds and the purling waters in the stream.

I see the blossoms of clovers, violets, and wild roses. I look carefully for the first signs of Queen Anne's lace and the gold of the marsh marigold by the spring on the steep side hill. My walks take me to the swamp where the alders and pussy willows thrive and where the pond lilies float on the placid waters.

My ears delight to the exuberant bird-songs of late spring. I hear the field and vesper sparrows and listen to the meadowlark perched on a fence post along the road. I may hear the whisper of a wind sending the timothy into rhythmic undulations in the old meadow.

My walks become my sanctuary of peace, a peace found in the hills and valleys and along the streams. Here I find the joy and pleasure I need as I follow my long pathway through the pages of time.

The author of three books, Lansing Christman has contributed to Ideals *for almost thirty years. Mr. Christman has also been published in several American, international, and braille anthologies. He lives in rural South Carolina.*

Vivid flowers gather at the edge of a creek near Imogene Pass in Colorado. Photo by Daniel Dempster.

The Weaver, May

Stella Craft Tremble

The weaver, May, before her loom
Began to weave the weather.
For warp and woof she used sunbeams
And songs of birds together.
From out her weft fell drops of pearls
To spangle reeds and rushes,
And then she whisked some silver notes
For morning song of thrushes.
She added hanks of fleecy skies
All banked with crystal edges,
Threw bolts of yellow daisies down
To trim the roadside hedges.
Her threads of iridescent light
Transformed the hill and heather.
May wound her shuttle with bouquets,
Loosed skeins of golden weather.

A hammock in Bashon, Washington, offers a spectacular ocean view. Photo by Jessie Walker.

84

Readers' Forum

Snapshots from Our Ideals Readers

Top right: Dale and Barbara Pedersen of Hammondsport, New York, share this photo of their three-year-old granddaughter Ashlyn Amsden, who is thrilled that a butterfly has decided to pause for a rest on her hand.

Lower left: Margaret Catherine Campbell, age one, is surrounded by a sea of ivy geraniums in this snapshot sent to us by her grandmother, Josephine Campbell of Great Falls, Virginia.

Lower right: Thirteen-month-old Jenna Briann Trantham comes upon a basket of flowers during her garden walk. Jenna is the great-granddaughter of Emily Stutts of Robbins, North Carolina.

Top left: Three-year-old Mia Tell thinks her first umbrella is quite special, both indoors and out. Mia is the daughter of Tamecca Chapman of Fort Wayne, Indiana.

Middle left: Six-year-old Mikelyn Olsen finds that flowers from Grandma definitely smell sweet. Mikelyn's proud grandmother is Helen Olsen of East Troy, Wisconsin.

Lower left: Margarita Messersmith of Silver Spring, Maryland, shares this photo of her granddaughter, Rita Cordero. Rita lives in Venezuela, where she loves to practice her cooking.

THANK YOU Dale and Barbara Pedersen, Josephine Campbell, Emily Stutts, Tamecca Chapman, Helen Olsen, Margarita Messersmith, Helen Hanson, Val Keinert, Virginia Anderson, and Carol and George Labadie for sharing your family photographs with *Ideals*. We hope to hear from other readers who would like to share snapshots with the *Ideals* family. Please include a self-addressed, stamped envelope if you would like the photos returned. Keep your original photographs for safekeeping and send duplicate photos along with your name, address, and telephone number to:

Readers' Forum
Ideals Publications
535 Metroplex Drive, Suite 250
Nashville, Tennessee 37211

Above: Young Alan Hanson admires the roses in the garden he shares with his grandmother, Helen Hanson of Shelton, Washington.

Lower left: Daniel Keinert, age two years, discovers bubbles with his nana, Val Keinert of Santa Maria, California.

Lower center: Virginia Anderson of Milton, Wisconsin, shares this photo of her two-year-old grandson, Samuel Wade, as he gets a close look at his great-grandmother, Lillian Greenman. Lillian is an amazing 101 years of age.

Lower right: Twenty-two-month-old Matt Cappo enjoys a laugh with his great-grandmother, Mary F. Labadie. The snapshot was sent to us by Matt's grandparents, Carol and George Labadie of Wayne, New Jersey.

ideals

Publisher, Patricia A. Pingry
Editor, Michelle Prater Burke
Managing Editor, Peggy Schaefer
Designer, Marisa Calvin
Copy Editor, Melinda Rathjen
Permissions, Patsy Jay
Contributing Editors, Lansing Christman and Pamela Kennedy

ACKNOWLEDGMENTS

BROOKS, GWENDOLYN. "Tommy" from *Bronzeville Boys and Girls.* Copyright © 1956 by Gwendolyn Brooks Blakely. Used by permission of HarperCollins Publishers. JAQUES, EDNA. "Mother's Smile" from *The Golden Road* and "Things They'll Remember" from *Backdoor Neighbors.* Used by permission of Thomas Allen & Son, Limited, Canada. RICHARDSON, ISLA PASCHAL. "A Far-Off Reason" from *Along the Way.* Copyright © 1962, Published by Bruce Humphries, Boston. Used by permission of Branden Books, Boston. STOFFEL, BETTY. "A Mother's Prayer." Used by permission of E. Lee Stoffel. THOMAS, ESTHER KEM. "Spring" and "Florist." Used by permission of Frederick A. Thomas. TOTH, SUSAN ALLEN. "Early Spring" from *Blooming: A Smalltown Girlhood.* Copyright © 1978 and 1981 by Susan Allen Toth. Published by Little, Brown and Company. Reprinted by permission of Aaron M. Priest Literary Agency, Inc. Our sincere thanks to the following authors and heirs whom we were unable to locate: Vera B. Hammann for "Spring" from *Sky Writing,* Leeward Publishing, Washington, DC; The Estate of Edna Greene Hines for "Out of the Past" from *White Butterflies;* The Estate of Helen Loomis Linham for "If You Grow a Garden"; The Estate of Kathleen Norris for "The Old, Dear Right"; The Estate of George N. Rees for "May Music"; Strickland Gillilan for "The Reading Mother" from *Best Loved Poems of the American People.*

NOTHING IS IMPOSSIBLE WITH — A LITTLE FAITH

"I tell you the truth, if you have faith as small as a mustard seed, you can say to this mountain, 'Move from here to there,' and it will move. Nothing will be impossible for you." — *Matthew 17:20*

SEEDS of FAITH
True Stories that Grew from Mustard Seeds

A Guideposts Exclusive

Jesus gave us many parables to make God's infinite wisdom accessible to ordinary people. One of the most powerful parables is that of the mustard seed. What a mighty message! Jesus also said, just as the mustard seed is the smallest of all seeds, yet grows into the largest of all garden plants, so it is with our faith and with the Kingdom of Heaven.

Now Guideposts has created two treasures to bring this enduring symbol of faith closer to home and closer to the heart. First there is a touching and encouraging book called, *Seeds of Faith: True Stories that Grew from Mustard Seeds*. It brings you stories from people for whom the mustard seed was a reminder of hope, inspiration, and the power of faith. The impact of these stories — and God's promise — will stay with you and give you a renewed sense of spiritual well-being.

Then, to help you carry the feelings of comfort and peace that you'll gain from reading those remarkable true stories, you can wear a special Guideposts custom-made *Mustard Seed Pendant Necklace*. The tiny mustard seed parable is a dynamic illustration of God's endless love and power. If we hold tight to this promise, we needn't be concerned or discouraged by our own abilities or boundaries. God will move the mountain.

The Necklace:
- Tear drop globe with encased mustard seed.
- 18" 24 kt gold-plated brass rope chain with deluxe lobster-claw clasp.
- Presented in an heirloom-quality black velvet gift box.

The Book:
- An enduring collection that will give you encouragement to face life's trials.
- Vivid examples of what the tiniest glimmer of faith can accomplish.
- 5" x 7 ½", 112 pages of joyful reading, bound in a sturdy, high-gloss printed case.

FREE EXAMINATION CERTIFICATE

YES! Please send my *Mustard Seed Pendant Necklace* and *Seeds of Faith* book to enjoy for 30 days risk-free. If I decide to keep the necklace and the book, I will pay the low Guideposts price of $19.96, payable in two easy installments of just $9.98, plus postage and handling. If not completely satisfied, I may return the necklace and book within 30 days and owe nothing. The FREE *Pocket Parable* is mine to keep, no matter what.
Total sets ordered: _____

Please print your name and address:

NAME _____

ADDRESS _____

CITY _____ STATE _____ ZIP _____

❏ Please Bill Me ❏ Charge My: ❏ MasterCard ❏ Visa

Credit Card #:

⬜⬜⬜⬜ ⬜⬜⬜⬜ ⬜⬜⬜⬜ ⬜⬜⬜⬜

Expiration Date: _____
Signature _____

Allow 4 weeks for delivery. Orders subject to credit approval.
Send no money now. We will bill you later.
www.guidepostsbooks.com

Printed in USA
011/202051102

Free

Just for ordering!

"I tell you the truth, if you have faith as small as a mustard seed, you can say to this mountain, 'Move from here to there', and it will move. Nothing will be impossible for you." — MATTHEW 17:20

When you reply today, we'll send you a FREE bonus gift — a special *Pocket Parable* card with the parable of the mustard seed printed on it. Yours to keep, no matter what.

NO NEED TO SEND MONEY NOW!